DOMENICK EPPS

WHOLESALE
TO
WEALTH

REAL ESTATE INVESTING BOOK

Wholesale To Wealth

DOMENICK EPPS, LLC

Suffolk, Virginia

ISBN: 979-8-9903284-0-2

Table Of Contents

Wholesale To Wealth

I WAS HOMELESS, SLEEPING IN MY CAR BUT GOD...

PLEASE READ THIS DISCLAIMER

Domenick Epps, is a licensed real broker with licenses in the States of Virginia, North Carolina and Georgia. The information provided in this book is for educational purposes only and do not reflect the teachings of the State of Virginia, the State of North Carolina or the State of Georgia Real Estate divisions nor does it reflect the National Association of Realtors. The information provided in this guide is not affiliated with Victory Allegiance Realty Inc. or A-Z Atlanta Realty LLC. Please consult with your financial and/or legal advisor prior to making any commitments mention within the pages of this book or any workshop/training associated.

As a licensed realtor I operate with a code of ethics. I must disclose to all potential clients my licensure status. Understanding most of you are not licensed, this book reflects to your situation as not being a licensed agent.

WELCOME BIRD DOGS

This book is intended to provide you with a thorough grasp of the wholesaling process in real estate, covering everything from vocabulary and fundamentals to advanced success strategies. Though this book does not cover everything in regards to wholesaling in real estate, it does cover a lot of ground and provide you with the tools and information you need to get started in this fast-paced business, regardless of your level of experience. Whether you're a newbie hoping to get into the real estate market or an experienced investor looking to improve your wholesaling abilities. If you know me, then you know that I hate procrastination.

So chances are, you received this book because you are HUNGRY and DETERMINED to be a successful real estate investor. And if that's the case get ready to to eat well.

I want to free some of you that are big on reaching and finishing books. Please do not treat this book like a novel. You do not have to read this from cover to cover. Treat this more as a workbook, so feel free to jump around to various chapters as needed.

Depending on where you are in your real estate investing career, you may not need all of the contents in this book. Maybe 1-3 chapters is all that you need, and that is ok. You will still be considered an alumni, even if you don't get to "complete" this book from cover to cover. No judgment zone here. Get what you need and get to work!

Learning Outcomes

After completing this read, you will:

· Have a Thorough Understanding of Real Estate Wholesaling

· Gain Insight into the Real Estate Market and Trends

· Effectively Locate and Analyze Distressed Properties

· Master the Art of Deal Analysis

· Acquire Essential Negotiation Techniques

· Navigate the Closing Process with Confidence

· Develop Effective Marketing and Branding Strategies

Introduction to Real Estate Wholesaling

So let's get right into what is wholesaling in real estate. Wholesaling is a strategy where as the investor you function as a liaison between a motivated seller and a possible end-buyer. You are the investor, not the buyer unless you choose to be both which is another discussion. I want to repeat that as the wholesaler you are the "investor" not the buyer. I know what you are thinking. You are thinking that it's the same thing, but actually it's not.

Trust me, I'm not trying to be deep, but I am trying to set the record straight that as a wholesaler you are not the buyer, unless you conduct a double closing which makes you the buyer and the seller. In other words, being a wholesaler mean that you are the "middleman/woman". Being the middle person is not a bad thing, it's actually a great thing as you will come to learn.

Wholesale To Wealth

You are the investor and you do not have to purchase the property in order to invest in the property. This is similar to stock options. You do not own the stock per se you own the contract and have an option to buy or sell that contract for a profit. You following me now? It's all about words and using the correct terminologies in the correct manner. I know that for the most part, you have heard a wholesaler say that they were making an cash offer to buy a property with a quick close. All of which are sayings we do not teach or recommend.

We do not advise anyone to say as a wholesaler that you are buying anything. We do not mention cash offers and we certainly do not communicate quick closings. Why is that? Because we understand that we need as much time as possible to market the property and get an actual buyer time to close and with title searches and inspections thats not a quick process.

Your first task as the wholesaler is to find properties that are distressed or undervalued, work up a purchase agreement with the seller at a reduced price, and then assign or resell the agreement to a final buyer, who is usually a fix-and-flipper or a buy and hold real estate investor.

Making a profit is what I would assume is your main goal of wholesaling. So starting out you may not want to spend money on mailers and all of the many platforms that are available to your disposal. I'm a firm believer of you having the business pay for itself with your operating expenses being at a minimum which also aims to speed up and streamline your property transactions.

Wholesaling requires legwork. It can create you some amazing opportunities but you have to make sure that you treat the business as a business by making sure that you're doing your business in your business. In other words, you should not be wholesaling in your personal name. Consult with an attorney or your CPA on the type of business to create before you start. I work with business owners, not hobbyist. I pour my passion into individuals who respect real estate investing as a business. I understand that everyone may not be afforded the opportunity to this do this full time, but even in your part time, you have to make sure that you treat this as a legitimate business. Therefore you will need at the least a business name, business license, EIN, and bank account.

Wholesaling in real estate requires minimal start up capital. The initial investment needed to enter into wholesaling is minimum as you do not have to make significant financial commitment to buy and renovate the properties you place under contract. Your expenses may range from $100 - $500 for starts, but you can really start wholesaling with zero out of pocket dollars. Tools such as a dialer system, CRM, skip

Wholesale To Wealth

tracing, mailers and ads all are essential but not required. Another reason that wholesaling in real estate in profitable is because you do not actually purchase the properties. Because of that, you are not subject to the risks that comes with real estate ownership. You do not have to worry about carrying costs, unexpected repairs or changes in the market.

Once you place a property under contract, you are considered the "contract owner". As the contract owner, you have the right to assign that contract to an end buyer who would then take on all of the risk associated with property ownership.

Please check with your local codes and restrictions as some states are requiring wholesalers to have their real estate license in order to conduct business. Also if you are a licensed real estate agent remember that you DO have to disclose that to the property owner.

DO YOU NEED MONEY RIGHT NOW?

I know the title of this chapter may seem a little off to some. I know it may seem like a very dumb question as we all are wholesaling in real estate to make money. But the question of do you need money right now is a very important question. People that are in dire need of money normally make poor decisions when there is a urgency to pay a bill for instance. When you are dealing with people and their resources, you do not want enter into this business out of desperation.

Wholesaling in real estate takes time. It's going to take time to master the craft and it is going to take time for the property that you do get under contract to get to the closing table. I know people tend to market quick closings, but it is less likely to be finished with a transaction quickly. There are steps that you are going to have to take before you get paid.

The only way to really get a quick closing as a wholesaler is if you get a property under contract in one day, already have a cash buyer with an expedited title search and no other contingencies. I'm not going to say that's impossible, but the likelihood of that really happening is slim.

So we do not recommend that you try to entice property owners by saying you can close quickly unless you are 99.9% sure that you can close quickly...and even then PLEASE DO NOT SAY IT because anything could happen and I've learned not to count closings until the deal has closed and funded.

If by all means possible when negotiating your offer to the seller, give yourself ample amount of time to close. Why? Because after you get the property under contract you have to be able to market the property and give the end buyer a due diligence period to conduct inspections and title searches. So as you can see, quick is not always true.

What Is The First Move

So to address the question of what you should do first, I'm going to treat this as if I'm speaking to a young rising high school graduate. Let's say you are working with a very minimum budget. Your first assignment is to establish your support list. This support list is going to be the catalyst to you building an extensive network of buyers and sellers in your area.

I call this support list **The Big 300**. The Big 300 is a spreadsheet for you to create of a minimum of 300 contacts that consists of family, friends, co-workers, classmates, neighbors and any one that you can call and share your vision of being a successful real estate investor to. These 300 people is who you are going to call on to be your extra eyes and ears in the marketplace.

It's important to communicate to them that you are investing in real estate and that you need their **support** in order to be successful. The key word here is support. Most people don't mind supporting someone that ask. But you must ASK and not allow fear or pride to stand in the way of you asking them for support.

Your goal is to have them to send you pictures of for sale by owner signs, addresses and pictures of homes that look unattended to along with anyone that they know that is buying real estate. If they have a friend that they know is investing in buying houses, you need them to connect you so that you can add them to your buyer's list. Is your cousin a home health care provider? Maybe she know of a family that is looking to sell their parents home? All the help you need is right there in your circle, you just have to ask them to help and most would love to help.

Sample The Big 300 Script:

You: Hey Aunt Tammy I'm reaching out to you because I need your help. NO, I'm not calling for money (giggles). I'm actually calling because I'm starting my career in real estate and one of my first assignments is reaching out to family and friends that is willing to support me in my efforts of being successful.

Aunt Tammy: Sure baby what you need!

You: Thank you! I just need your eyes, ears and fingers. If you happen to ride pass a home that looks abandoned or unattended to, may you send me a picture of it along with the address? Also if you hear of someone that is looking to sell or purchase a home, could you be sure to give them my contact information and ask if it was ok for you to give me theirs?

This network of supporters will provide you with opportunities for repeat business and as your business expands you may be willing to throw in a referral fee or some gesture of thanks.

You want to spend the first three weeks of keeping in contact with **The Big 300**. The initial contact should be a phone call, but after that just send out weekly check-ins. The group of leads that you receive from your group of supporters are the ones that you want to contact first.

Most of you have at least 300 contacts in your phone. Start there!

After you have exhausted all of your close contacts then and only then reach out to your social media contacts.

Subject A is 1,500 sq ft. 3 bedrooms 1 full and 1 half bath.

YOU OFFER $110,000
SELLER COUNTERED AT $115,000

YOU ARE UNDER CONTRACT AT $115,000

YOUR CONTRACT IS FOR 60 DAYS

ARV IS $265,000

If you get the end buyer to purchase this property for $125,000 and you close before the expiration date, you just made $10,000. You see how this works!

What's Your Target Market

If you are going to be a successful wholesaler it's important for you to establish and develop a keen understanding of your target market. By establishing your market you are positioning yourself for lucrative opportunities. So where should you target first? If you are on the East Coast should your target audience be on the West Coast? If you are in Georgia should your target audience be property owners in New York? Absolutely not! Think about this right quick before you continue.

What areas do you know like the back of your hand? What neighborhoods are you the most familiar with?

Wholesale To Wealth

Answer the following you are the most familiar with:

1. Street _____
2. Neighborhood _____
3. Zip Code _____
4. City _____

Don't make the mistake of trying to make phone calls all over the world or drive for dollars from state to state. Can you be in one region and conduct transactions in another? You absolutely can. I've had one wholesaler that sold me a property in downtown Suffolk, Virginia while he was in West Virginia. So the answer is yes, if you are more familiar with a specific area, even though it's not where you currently reside.

While we recommend that you start with an area you are the most familiar with and an area where people are the most familiar with you; if you are not located in that area then you will need to partner with someone that will be available to conduct your walkthroughs.

Even if you moved away from your hometown, make calls to property owners in your hometown because the saying is true "there's no place like home."

It's important that you target specific neighborhoods or regions where you have some traction already. Maybe it's where you grew up, went to school, attended church or worked. Starting in a region that you are the most familiar with just gives you the upper hand. You should already know what homes are really selling for in that area and what homes are the most abandoned.

So an ideal situation is that you are starting in an area that you are the most familiar with and that is an area where you currently reside or in close proximity to drive to once an appointment is made. Remember that in anything that you do that you will only get out what you put in it. So if you are going to be a successful real estate wholesaler, then you must be committed and remain consistent. Procrastination cannot be a character trait.

Wholesale To Wealth

One of the lessons my mentor Toney Black gave me early on in my real estate career centered around the word "obsession". He shared with me that in order for me to be successful in real estate I had to become obsess. I needed to eat, sleep and everything else real estate. And he was right.

As real estate wholesaler you play a critical role in the transaction process. You are essentially matchmakers, connecting sellers with motivated buyers.

Your key responsibilities and functions:

• **Lead Generation**: Actively seeking out distressed or undervalued properties that have the potential for a profitable wholesale deal.

• **Building Relationships:** Cultivating relationships with sellers & buyers to create a reliable network for future transactions.

• **Contract Assignment:** After ratifying a legally binding contract with the seller your next assignment is to market that property so subsequently you are assigning that contract to the end buyer.

• **Negotiation Skills:** Engaging with sellers to negotiate favorable purchase contracts, often at prices below the property's market value.

• **Market Analysis:** Conducting thorough market research to determine the After Repair Value (ARV) and Maximum Allowable Offer (MAO) for a given property.

• **Problem-Solving:** Addressing challenges or obstacles that may arise during the transaction process, such as title issues or unforeseen repairs.

Wholesale To Wealth

In essence, as a real estate wholesaler you are acting as the linchpin that brings together motivated sellers and eager buyers, creating a win-win situation for all parties involved including yourself. You have the ability to do all of this from the comfort of your home or office.

The majority of your business will consist of phone calling; initial phone calls and follow-up calls. Consider yourself setting up a money making call center in your home before you think about out-sourcing this task to virtual assistants. Trust me when I say, I know there are people that talk about out-sourcing, but why would you want someone to make the connection with your clients?

Trust and believe that regardless of what others think you got this. There is something in you that says as Eric Thomas aka ET The Hip-Hop Preacher puts it **"I CAN, I WILL, I MUST BE SUCCESSFUL"**

I WANT TO EMPHASIZE THAT JUST ABOUT EVERY MAJOR CORPORATION IS A WHOLESALER AND WE ALL PARTICIPATE IN THE WHOLESALE BUSINESS. AMAZON, WALMAT, TARGET AND EVEN YOUR LOCAL CONVENIENCE STORES ARE WHOLESALERS.

THEY ALL ACQUIRE GOODS FOR ONE AMOUNT AND RESALE IT FOR A PROFIT.

Key Vocabulary in Real Estate Wholesaling

Appraisal - An estimate or opinion of a property's value; also refers to the report that includes supporting evidence of the opinion.

Appraiser - A qualified professional who conducts an appraisal. Appreciation - An increase in the market value of a property due to market conditions or property improvements.

ARV (After Repair Value) - The after repair value (ARV) of a property is its current worth after any necessary repairs, renovations, or enhancements have been made. It is an essential indicator for wholesalers as it indicates a property's possible resale value.

Assignee - The person to whom something is assigned.

Assignment - The transfer of a contract or right from one person to another.

Assignment Agreement – Agreement between the buyer and seller where the buyer agrees to buy a property for a set fee. Assignment Agreements are pivotal in wholesaling as they facilitate the transfer of the property contract without the wholesaler taking ownership. This allows for a seamless transaction process.

Assignor - The party who makes an assignment.

Bilateral Contract - A binding agreement between two parties where they both exchange promises to perform and fulfill one side of a bargain.

Bill of Sale - The written instrument which transfers title to personal property.

Carrying Costs – Expenses incurred on a property over the course of owning it. These costs usually include utilities, debt service payments, taxes and insurance, security, etc.

Chain of Title - The history of all the documents on record having transferred title to a particular property starting with the earliest document and ending with the most recent.

Clear Title - One that is free of any clouds of defects.

Closing / Settlement - The finalization of a real estate and/or financing transaction which involves applying the various costs, credits and prorations to the appropriate parties and signing all required documents in the presence of an attorney or closing agent.

Closing Agent - The person or business entity that coordinates a closing. The closing agent will prepare the closing documents and disburse funds. A closing agent could be a title company or an attorney.

Closing Costs - Fees such as loan origination, title search, survey, attorney and prepaid items such as escrow deposits for taxes and insurance in connection with a real estate/financing transaction.

Closing Date - The date on which a real estate and/or financing transaction is finalized. The date on which a closing occurs.

Closing Statement - A detailed account used in the final settlement of a real estate transaction that shows all amounts paid by or due to each party. Also called a settlement statement.

Cloud on title - An outstanding claim or encumbrance which may not be valid, but would affect or impair the condition of a title.

Competitive Market Analysis (CMA) - A method of estimating a property's worth by comparing it with properties that are currently on the market or have sold recently; an informal appraisal.

Contingency - When one event is dependent upon the happening of another event. For example: a buyer would not have to go through with a purchase contract if the contract was contingent upon the buyer obtaining a mortgage loan that he or she was unable to obtain.

Convey - To transfer ownership of something or title to something.

Conveyance - The transfer of title to real estate through a deed or some other instrument.

Corporate Resolution - A declaration to do or not to do something as voted on by the officers of a corporation. This document is required if you are buying or selling in your business name.

Correction deed - The recording of a deed for the sole purpose of correcting an inaccuracy in an earlier recording such as a misspelled name or an inaccurate property description.

Counteroffer - A rejection of an offer accompanied by a new offer which better suits the original offeree's needs. An offer made in response to an offer received.

Deed - The instrument used to convey title to real property from one party (the grantor) to another party (the grantee); the instrument which is evidence of ownership.

Deposit - Money given as evidence of good faith; earnest money.

Due Diligence - A thorough investigation of a potential investment considering and confirming all material facts involved. The reasonable amount of care a person should take prior to entering into a contractual relationship with another party

Earnest Money - Money offered as good faith usually paid with an offer to purchase; a deposit.

Encroachment - A building, fence or other improvement which extends beyond the boundary line of the property it is erected upon and intrudes onto the neighboring property.

Equity - The value of a property over and above the total amount of any mortgages or other liens against it.

Escrow - is a third-party neutral service that keeps and handles finances and documents associated with a real estate transaction. It guarantees that all contract criteria are satisfied before the property is transferred.

Flipping – Purchasing a property with the intention to sell for a profit. Property may or may not require a renovation before reselling

Lease Option & Assignment – Purchasing a property on a lease where the monthly payments go towards the option to buy the property.

Lien - A right given by law to a creditor to have a debt or charge paid out of the property or proceeds from the sale of property belonging to the debtor; a hold or claim on property as security which becomes an encumbrance on that property.

MAO (Maximum Allowable Offer) - MAO represents the highest price you as the wholesaler can pay for a property while still maintaining a viable profit margin. It is calculated by considering the ARV, estimated repair costs, and desired profit margin.

Marketable Title - Salable title; clear; free of defects.

Mechanics Lien - A specific lien in favor of an unpaid contractor or material supplier who has erected or repaired a building or other improvement to real estate.

Open Listing - A listing agreement that gives the broker a nonexclusive right to secure a buyer. It may be given to any number of brokers at the same time with the seller obligated to pay a commission only to one who actually finds a buyer.

Purchase and Sale Agreement - A contract between a buyer and seller that details all of terms of a sale such as purchase price, earnest money deposit, down payment, financing terms, closing date contingencies, etc.

Quitclaim Deed - An instrument used to clear or convey, without warranties, a questionable claim a person may have to a title.

Real Estate Commission - A state governmental agency charged with the responsibility of protecting the general public through the enforcement of laws and promulgation of regulations dealing with the activities or real estate licensees. The Real Estate Commission also issues licenses and if necessary takes disciplinary action against licensees or revokes licenses.

Release - The discharge of an obligation or responsibility; to relinquish a right claim or interest. If you as the wholesaler is not able to close on a property you would send over a release document to release you from all obligations and to have the escrow agent to "release" back to you or the end-buyer the EMD payment.

Wholesale To Wealth

Seller Motivation - The fundamental reasons why a property owner is eager or motivated to sell their property. Financial difficulty, personal situations, or a need for an immediate sale can all be sources of motivation. Recognizing seller motivation allows you to tailor your approach to present offers that meet the specific needs and priorities of the seller. This can lead to more favorable deal negotiations.

Skip Tracing - is the process of locating individuals or property owners whose contact information is not readily available. There are certain programs to use that will assist you locating motivated sellers or potential buyers. Effective skip tracing techniques will enable you to identify and reach out to property owners, even if they have limited or outdated contact information. This expands the pool of potential deals.

Title Company - is a specialized agency responsible for conducting title searches, examining public records, and issuing title insurance policies.

Warranty Deed - Full covenant and warranty deed - A deed in which the grantor makes the warranties of seisin, against encumbrances, quiet enjoyment, further assurances, and warranty forever. Before title insurance was widely used grantees needed to rely on the warranties made by the grantor if the title proved to be defective.

These important terms are essential for comprehending and managing real estate wholesaling. These serve as the foundation for making educated choices and carrying out beneficial deals. There are many other terms that you will need to know but these are a start for you.

DISC ASSESSMENT

A **i** person in the DiSC quadrant places emphasis on **influencing** or persuading others. They tend to be enthusiastic, optimistic, open, trusting, and energetic.

Individuals with an high **"I"** scores tend to be great when it comes to making the calls but this next session we will discover leans more towards those in the high C category.

Conscientiousness: A person in the DiSC quadrant places emphasis on quality, accuracy, expertise and competency.

The above comes from the DiSC Profile Website. Conduct your DiSC assessment by visiting the website below.

https://www.discprofile.com/what-is-disc/disc-styles

Analyzing Your Market

This chapter is for those of you who loves data and loves research. So if you are an high "i" you need to either get someone on your team that enjoys doing the research or you are going to have to pump your breaks and do what you don't enjoy doing. Dharius Daniels teaches us that you don't go as far as your dream, you go as far as your team. I'm grateful to have partners like Randall and Ava that enjoys doing the research.

Being able to analyze the real estate market is foundational to successful wholesaling. It allows you to strategically target your efforts, identify lucrative opportunities, and make informed decisions about which properties to pursue. This knowledge empowers you to navigate the market with confidence and increase your chances of profitability.

If you are going to succeed as a real estate investor, you need to learn how to analyze the market.   Market research and analysis involves systematic gathering, interpretation, and evaluation of data related to a specific market or geographical area. This process will help you to make informed decisions about which properties to pursue and how to approach potential deals.

Through market research, you can pinpoint neighborhoods or regions where there is a high concentration of distressed or undervalued properties. These properties may have high to 100% equity creating potential opportunities for profitable wholesaling deals. There are softwares such as PropStream that can assist with market research.

Investing in real estate is not something to take likely. Most people enter into this field without properly mitigating risk. Risk mitigation is a proactive approach that consists of a thorough analysis that helps in assessing the level of risk associated with a particular market. This includes factors like property values, historical appreciation rates, and economic stability. Researching market trends is what allows you to stay attuned to what moves the market such as shifts in property values, demand for certain types of properties, and emerging neighborhoods.

Wholesale To Wealth

The neighborhood that you grew up in is the neighborhood you should know more than anyone else. You should become familiar with what the rental rates are, what the resale values are, and who is looking to sell their home. If the neighborhood that you grew up in is a rent heavy neighborhood then more than likely those homes have lots of equity, especially if the owners of up in age.

Have you ever heard the saying "jack of all trades and master of none"? Well in real estate investing you want to learn how to concentrate your efforts in specific areas that you can become experts in. Instead of trying to be all over the place in every market in America, focus your analysis on a specific market. Gain intimate knowledge on the property values, buyer preferences, and local dynamics in that market. By doing so you will become an efficient resource.

Focusing on target areas allows you to allocate your time, energy, and resources to build strong networks with local stakeholders and become well-acquainted with the market's intricacies. Working within defined target areas increases the likelihood of finding multiple deals in close proximity, enabling you to increase your deal volume and profitability.

It's important that you are constantly monitoring the trends and demands in the real estate market as it tends to change like the seasons. This involves staying updated on shifts in buyer preferences, as it's important for you to know the types and price range of properties your investors are interested in.

For instance, some investors only want to purchase multi-family homes while others only want single family homes. Just about every wholesaler that sends us properties know that I prefer to purchase at a price no more than 45-50% of the ARV. So it's imperative that you have great notes in your CRM in regards to what a specific investor is looking for. Don't assume that every real estate investor is the same because that is certainly not the case. When you are aware of the demands in the market, that information alone will assist you with being precise and therefore a much better birddog.

Demographic changes, and economic factors also influence property values and investment potential. Being aware of these trends and demand patterns allows you to adapt your strategy to meet changing market conditions. For instance, if there is a surge in demand for multi-family properties, you can adjust your focus accordingly and spend more time calling multi-family owners. Knowledge of current demand helps you to align your acquisitions with what buyers are actively seeking, increasing the likelihood of successful transactions.

As a wholesaler that understands the market, you will be able to effectively work the market.. You do not have to be a jack of all trades. Focus, focus, focus and get to work on your market, in your market and be the expert of the market.

WOULD YOU LIKE TO TAKE YOUR REAL ESTATE INVESTING CAREER TO THE NEXT LEVEL?

OF COURSE YOU DO

Due to the rising changes in legislation we are recommending all wholesalers to get their real estate license. Trust me, having your license is going to take your investment career to another level giving you access and tools most investors long for. The one school where you can get the education and preparation you need in-person or virtually is Moseley Real Estate.

MOSELEY®
Real Estate Schools
https://moseley.org/

Finding Distressed Properties Strategies

Now it's time to target a specific area in your research. You do not have to call every property owner on your street or in your neighborhood. For instance, why would you call the property owner that just closed last month on their new home? You wouldn't call them nor would you call someone that just refinanced their home and their new mortgage is at the top of the value.

You want to find distressed properties. A distressed property refers to a property that is either in pre-foreclosure status, foreclosure, or bank owned. A distressed property may not necessarily be a dilapidated property which is a property that is in the state of disrepair. A property becomes "distressed" when the owner falls behind on their mortgage payments and/or property tax bills. Finding distressed properties have become much easier with technology.

There are several ways to identify distress properties. Below is a few ways to identify them:

- Driving for Dollars
- Websites
- Local Auctions
- County Tax Records Court Records
- News / Obituaries
- Bankruptcy/Divorce Attorney
- Code Enforcement

It's important to note that the majority of distressed property owners may not be in the best emotional state to discuss their situation. Showing empathy is key here if you are going to convert and close the deal. You do not want to display overly aggressive behavior as that is a turn off.

Now let's look into some strategies to find these distressed properties. What are some tactics that you can use to assist you in getting properties possibly under contract and closed.

Direct Mail Campaigns Strategy: Utilizing direct mail marketing allows you to reach out to property owners who may be motivated to sell. This involves sending personalized letters or postcards offering to buy their property.

Networking Strategy: Building strong relationships within the real estate community, including realtors, investors, and bankruptcy and divorce attorneys, can lead to referrals for potential deals.

Online Real Estate Platforms Strategy: Websites and platforms dedicated to real estate listings, such as Zillow, Redfin, and Realtor.com, can be used to search for distressed properties.

Driving for Dollars Strategy: Physically driving through neighborhoods, looking for signs of distress such as overgrown yards, boarded-up windows, or neglected properties is an hands-on approach that can lead to the discovery of potential deals. Now with technology you can drive for Dollars Virtually. using Google Maps.

Public Records and Foreclosure Listing Strategy: Accessing public records and foreclosure listings can provide valuable information about properties facing financial challenges or in foreclosure proceedings such as Zillow Pre-Foreclosure listings.

Finding distressed properties is a critical aspect of successful real estate wholesaling. You may also find distressed properties on the MLS but if it's on the market, chances are there is less room for negotiations and you do not want to be in a tight situation with an agent or seller.

Marketing Techniques for Leads

Now let's talk marketing techniques for you to implement as a means to gather leads or potential clients. Marketing is one key component to wholesaling. You not only have to market yourself as the brand but you will also have to market the property once you get it under contract.

Here is where you will solicit the help of **The Big 300**. You are going to need your group of supporters to help market you as a real estate professional and the properties that you have under contract. Just imagine how far your reach will be if you had just 50 people making a post about your real estate business. There are ways to market organically and your group of supporters is the best place to start.

Now apart from your group of supporters, let's discuss other ways to market yourself and to market your properties.

Having a professional website and/or social media profile dedicated to real estate investing can establish credibility and make it easier for potential leads to find and contact you. Believe it or not but property owners will go searching and one of the easiest places to start is your social media page. They want to know that you are who you say you are and if your pages don't align with their values you may lose a deal.

Be sure to optimize your online content for search engines as that can increase the visibility of your website or online presence, making it easier for potential leads to discover you. Providing valuable content through blogs, videos, reels or webinars related to real estate and wholesaling can attract leads looking for information and build trust.

Should I have a separate business page from my personal?

That question gets ask a lot in regards to social media platforms. The issue with that question is that most people believe that clients only go to their business page, when in fact most people are going to check whatever is associated with your name. Now, if you have an alias and you are not using your government name then you should be fine. But in my case, my name is my brand. So I have my name for all social media platforms as well as my website which makes it easier for clients and potential clients to find me.

Your social media platforms doesn't only have to have real estate content. You just have to be ok with your clients viewing your content. Some of you don't post much anyway but for the younger generation this is really crucial for you. Engaging with potential leads on platforms like LinkedIn, Facebook, Instagram and TikTok can help establish connections and generate interest in your services along with using correct hashtags on all of your posts.

Social Media: Have a professional photo and use your business card or company logo as your cover image. Also create educational content in regards to different real estate investing topics. Create reels of you going in and out of homes, walkthroughs, inspections, and especially CLOSINGS!

Business Cards and Printed Material: Have a professional business card that have your contact info but not your personal address. Use a virtual address. A co-working space would be great because if they want to research your business address they will see an actual building and not your home.

Blast your business cards and printed materials all over the town and use **The Big 300** to assist you with this effort.

Analyzing Deals: Calculating After Repair Value (ARV)

What makes a deal an actual good deal is the numbers. I'm sure you've heard the saying BUY LOW & SELL HIGH, and that is the absolute truth. As a wholesaler your number one objective is to get the property under contract at the lowest price possible. But how do you get to that low price without "disrespecting" the property owner while also making sure that you are not over-paying for a property? One of the ways that you do so is by first determining the ARV also known as the After Repair Value.

The **ARV** is an estimate of the market value of a property after it has undergone necessary repairs, renovations, or improvements. It represents the potential resale value of the property in its improved condition based on recent sold comparable properties.

Determining the ARV is a critical factor in assessing the potential profitability of a wholesale transaction. To determine the ARV you are going to research and use 3-4 comparable SOLD properties within a one-mile radius also known as "comps" that sold in less than a one year. These properties need to be similar in location, size, and amenities. It will not be similar in condition as your subject property may not be full renovated. Also if your subject property is a ranch one-story home, you would not use a two-story property. If your subject property was built in 1950 you would not use a new construction property as one of your comps.

The properties that you choose should be within the same neighborhood or same type of neighborhood and bridges and tracks are normal indicators of those neighborhood changes.

A point to remember is that when choose comps for your ARV you can always go down but you cannot go up. to be more specific this means that you can use a hood comp for a suburban subject if need be, but you cannot use a suburban property for a hood subject property. You can use a one story comp for a two story subject but you cannot use a two story comp for a one story subject.

To locate these properties you may use real estate websites such as Zillow, Redfin, Realtor.com and/or your local MLS provider. You may reach out to a real estate professional such as a real estate broker who can provide a comparable market analysis also known as a CMA report or real estate appraiser is one sure way to get the fair market value.

This is why having your real estate license is a plus. Because you will be able to use the MLS to put together your CMA report as some of these websites may not have up-to-date data. Understanding that most of you reading this book may not have your real estate license and/or access to the MLS, I'm going to provide you with some quick DIY steps.

One of my partners upon knowing about this book could not believe that I was willing to share all of this information LOL. Well, I did because we want to see you WIN and WIN BIG.

Visit www.zillow.com/homes/

1. Type in the subject property address that you are searching [City, Neighborhood, ZIP, Address Q]

2. Write down all of the key data of the property: bedroom #, bath #, Sq.ft, acres, stories, type of the subject property. This information may vary if the subject property had bedrooms or baths added that was not reported to its county/city real estate accessors office.

3. Screen Print the information. If you are using a Mac computer for your screen print option hold down shift-command-4 and you can draw out the items that you want to capture for reference back to the subject properties or emailing your partners. Using a pc Capture the image — Assuming the area you want to capture is displayed on your screen, press the Print Screen (often shortened to "PrtScn") key, typically located in the upper-right corner of your keyboard, to capture a screenshot of your entire display. This normally goes to your documents folder or iCloud desktop.

4. Under Listing Type click on RECENTLY SOLD

5. Set min price to the average price of homes for sale in that area or from one of the lowest price homes pre-generated. Depending on the property style and the neighborhoood make-up you may have to reduce your min price average.

6. Set Beds to 2+ or 3+ depending on the property or what the investor is looking to do to the property. Remember this is After Repair Value, so you are looking for current homes that sold for what you

7. Adjust home type to the type of home that the subject property and deselect all others.

8. Under More- Start with sold in last 6 months and adjust up if you need more.

Home Type (1) ^   Mo

Home Type

✓ **Select All**

☑ Houses

☐ Townhomes

☐ Multi-family

☐ Condos/Co-ops

☐ Lots/Land

☐ Apartments

☐ Manufactured

Apply

Number Of Stories
☐ Single-story only

Senior Living
☐ Hide 55+ communities

Other Amenities
☐ Must have A/C
☐ Must have pool
☐ Waterfront

View
☐ City
☐ Mountain
☐ Park
☐ Water

Sold In Last
✓ Any
1 day
7 days
14 days
30 days
90 days
6 months
12 months
24 months
36 months

9. You can remove the pre established boundary that is created and draw your own radius. Use this feature if you are familiar with the area and know which streets are comparable to the subject property neighborhood make-up.

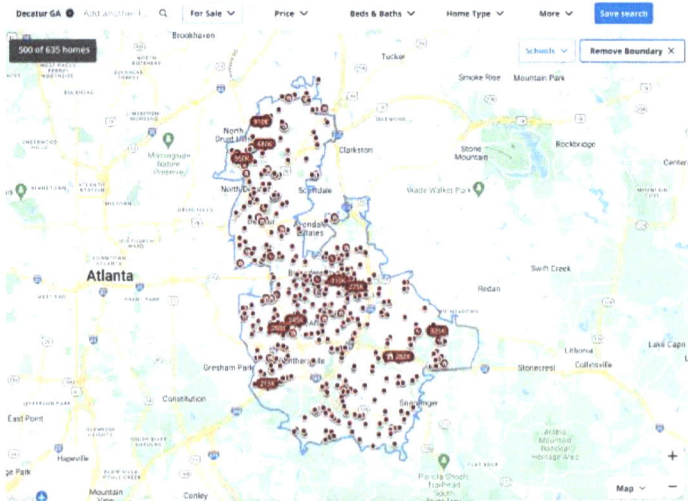

* Note that if you see red then you're looking at the For Sale and not the "SOLD" homes. So be sure to change it to SOLD and then adjust so that you are within a one mile radius.

10. Next you want to write down the information of 3-4
properties that is comparable to your subject property. You
want these homes to be within a one-mile radius and
comparable to your subject property.

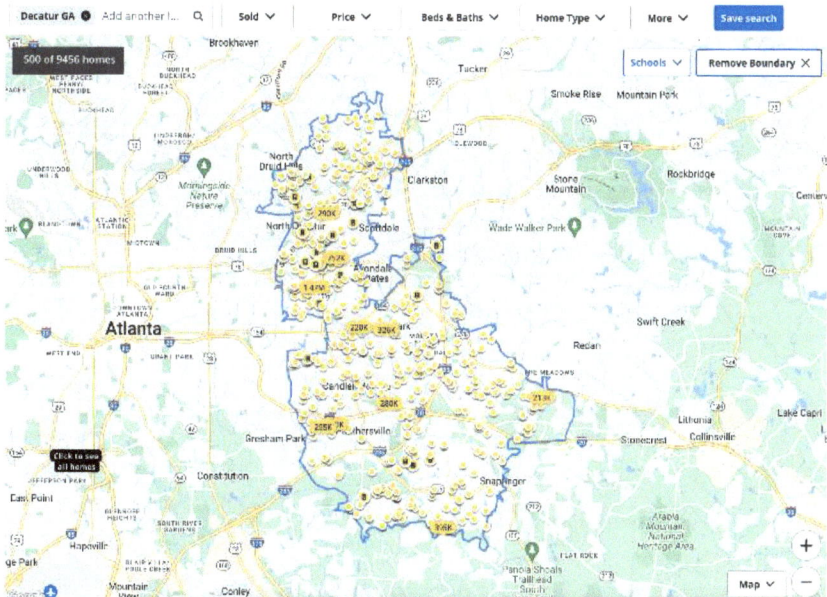

*Comparable does not mean that you want to find a home in the same
condition. If the subject property needs work, you do not want to use that
as a comp when determining ARV. You want finished homes.*

11. Add up the sold price and divide it by the number of properties and that will equal the ARV.

Add all 4 properties $999,400

Divide by number of properties (4)

ARV= $249,850

Sold 02/06/2024
$227,000
3 bds 2 ba -- sqft - Sold

Sold 02/13/2023
$217,400
3 bds | 2 ba | 1,057 sqft - Sold

Sold 10/03/2023
$270,000
3 bds 1.5 ba 1,531 sqft - Sold

Sold 08/03/2023
$285,000
3 bds 2 ba | 1,131 sqft - Sold

In some instances you may make price adjustments. Adjustments can be made for instance if one property has an extra bathroom, an in-ground pool instead of an above-ground pool, or some other type of amenity.

Analyzing Deals: Calculating Estimate Repair Cost

Now that you know how to determine the ARV, another tool is being able to determine the estimated repair cost. There are several ways that you can do so with of course the main sure way is to actually have at least three contractors to go out and give you quotes. But the reality is, as a wholesaler you don't have time to do all of that so you have to use unconventional ways and we have a few formulas that you can use.

Square Footage Method: This is a sight unseen method that involves estimating repair costs based on the property's square footage. A typical range per square foot is used, which can vary depending on factors such as the extent of repairs needed and the local market.

For example, if the average repair cost per square foot in your area is $40, and the property is 2,000 square feet, the estimated repair cost would be $80,000. When using the square footage method keep in mind that the price per square feet ranges from cosmetic repairs such as paint, carpet cleaning and/or removal to major repairs such as new roof install, new hvac system and a full gut which would increase the price per square to almost double the cosmetic cost.

Itemized Checklist Method: This method involves creating a checklist of common repair items and their estimated costs. This could include categories such as roofing, plumbing, electrical, flooring, painting, kitchen upgrades, bathroom renovations, etc. Go through the property and estimate the cost of each repair item, then total the costs for an overall estimate.

Percentage of ARV Method: This method is another sight unseen method that you may use without physically walking through the property. This percentage can vary depending on factors such as the condition of the property from online pictures or photos you've taken while driving for dollars and the extent of renovations needed. For example, if the ARV of a property is $200,000 and the estimated repair costs are typically 20% of the ARV, the repair cost would be $40,000.

Contractor Estimates: Obtain 2-3 estimates from licensed contractors or professionals in the construction industry. They can provide detailed quotes based on a walkthrough of the property and the scope of work required. This method tends to be the most accurate but may require more time and effort. If the subject property has 2 bedrooms but all of the comps are 3 bedrooms then you will need to get a cost for either adding on another bedroom or being able to add a bedroom within the current framework of the property.

Software/Applications: There are various software programs and mobile applications designed specifically for estimating repair costs in real estate. These tools often provide templates, databases of common repair costs, and customizable features to tailor estimates to your specific property and location. Whichever method you choose, it's essential to be thorough and realistic in your assessment of repair costs to ensure accurate budgeting and planning for your real estate investment.

Regardless of what method you use, understand that the best way to determine the repair cost is to physically tour the home. Here you want to point out as many defects with the property as possible as this will help to justify your low offer.

Analyzing Deals: Determine Your Desired Profit

Let's get to the bag because that is the real reason why you got this book. Most people out the gate would just throw out a dollar amount, such as $10,000 or $25,000 per transaction without being flexible. What we train our buy & flip clients is for them to use an actual percentage instead of a flat dollar amount as for them using a percentage is what keeps them humble and it keeps them from missing out on good opportunities!

But with wholesaling it's different! You can actually go into a transaction with a fixed amount of money that you want from the transaction prior to doing any research. You get to set the fee. How many jobs do you know that will allow you to do just that? You get to set the fee... but just don't be stuck on the fee.

Wholesale To Wealth

You get to define how much of a profit you want to make off of each transaction. But your ability to be flexible on that amount is what will allow you to lower that amount if needed to get the deal to close. Your fixed number can be adjusted with each transaction.

You may have one deal that you charge a $5,000 assignment fee and then there may be another transaction where there is so much equity that you are able to get a $35,000 assignment fee. Just don't get caught up in the numbers that you are not bendable. Remember that you will not get paid if you are not able to assign the deal to an end buyer that actually closes. And you don't want to get stuck with a possible default suit because you didn't close and you didn't have the right verbiage to get you out of the deal.

We are all about goal setting and setting income goals. This business is one business where you can adjust your numbers at any given time. Just remember to focus on your numbers and not the sellers or the end-buyer. Don't let your pride get in the way when you are seeing how much the seller will make from the deal or the end-buyer when they flip the property.

If you are so concerned about the investor's and property owner's pockets maybe you should consider being the buyer and not just the wholesaler.

Analyzing Deals: Calculating Max Allowable Offer (MAO)

Determining the maximum allowable offer (MAO) represents the highest price you will pay for a property while still ensuring a viable profit margin. It is calculated by considering the above determining factors, including the ARV, estimated repair costs, and desired profit. The max offer is not an offer that you start with but an offer that in your negotiations you would be willing to escalate up to.

ARV - DESIRED PROFIT - REPAIR COST = MAO

Using this formual will assist you in ensuring that there is room on the table for an investor to make a profit as well. If the seller agrees to your lowest offer you can increase your assignment and then decrease as need be to keep the deal in tact.

The MAO helps to establish a threshold for how much can be invested in a property to mitigate the risk of overpaying and potentially eroding profits. Knowing the MAO guides you in making informed purchase decisions. It provides a clear benchmark for negotiations with sellers and helps avoid acquiring properties at unprofitable prices which in turn will keep you from being able to assign the property to an end-buyer. Calculating MAO ensures that there is enough room for profit after factoring in acquisition costs and repair expenses. If the seller agrees to your lowest offer, only then can you increase your assignment percentage and decrease it to keep the deal in tact.

Never communicate your Max Allowable Offer to the seller out the gate and never communicate "final offer" because you do not want to miss out on a transaction over a few bucks. Trust me that $2,000 still stings till this day as I made the mistake of saying final offer.

3 Reasons To Reduce Your Assignment Fee

1. **Increase Sales Volume:** By reducing the assignment fee, you can attract more buyers who may have been hesitant due to the high fee.

2. **Competitive Advantage**: Lowering the assignment fee can give you a competitive advantage in the market compared your competitors who have higher fees.

3. **Clear Excess Inventory** : Reducing your fee can help you clear out excess inventory and free up space for new products.

Wholesale Negotiating Techniques: Effective Communication

I'm sure you have heard the ABC phrase which stands for ALWAYS BE CLOSING. In order to be a successful closer you must be a strong negotiator and there are some tactics that you must initiate if you want to close the deal. One of those tactics is the ability to build rapport. Building rapport with sellers is the process of establishing a positive and trusting relationship that fosters open communication and mutual understanding.

Building rapport is the solid foundation for successful negotiations. If you are determined to be successful and well-respected as a real estate professional then it is imperative that you use the tools being mentioned in this chapter. Below are a few skill sets that will help **10x** your wholesale business.

Wholesale To Wealth

Active Listening: Pay close attention to what the seller is saying, demonstrate genuine interest, and ask clarifying questions to show that you value their perspective.

Demonstrate Empathy: Understand and acknowledge the seller's emotions and motivations. Showing empathy helps create a sense of trust and mutual understanding.

Open and Transparent Communication: Honesty does go a long way as it fosters a more collaborative negotiation process. It's okay to communicate that you are a real estate investor. You do not have to communicate that you are looking to purchase, but you can say that you are looking to invest. Sounds the same but it's not.

Respect Boundaries: Be mindful of the seller's personal space and privacy, creating a comfortable and non-invasive atmosphere.

Finding Common Ground: Identify shared interests or objectives to establish a sense of camaraderie and alignment, creating a more positive negotiation environment. Maybe you both have passion for the Lord or you both are into sports. There are cues that you would be able to pick up on very quickly.

Conveying Information Clearly: This involves clearly articulating your points and avoiding jargon or overly complex language to ensure that the seller(s) understands the terms and conditions of the negotiation and restate the seller's points. If you are negotiating in person pay close attention to body language, facial expressions, and tone of voice to gain additional insights into their emotions and intentions.

Ask Open-Ended Questions: This allows yourself to gather more helpful information. Instead of asking the question "would you like for me to call you back" which gives a yes or no answer; you would ask "what is the best time for me to give you call?" This question will open up a more detailed answer which uncovers valuable information such as what time they may get home from work, prepare dinner, etc.

Responding, Not Reacting: Take a moment to consider your response rather than reacting impulsively. This allows for more thoughtful and strategic communication. Most people want to spend time defending themselves but understand that it is ok to end a conversation without a deal today to restart the conversation on another day without bridges being burnt. So it's ok to say "I totally understand where you are coming from and I will follow up with you and check in from time to time."

SAYING "I'M A CASH BUYER"

When you're not is not cool. If you personally don't have
proof of funds, then don't say that you are a cash buyer.
There are people that say that and our opinion it doesn't help
to get the deal done because you are being untruthful.

SAYING "I CAN CLOSE QUICK"

Another pet peeve. Like how do you know how quick the
closing is going to be? We don't recommend this statement.

Wholesale Negotiating Techniques: Overcoming Objections

Anticipating objections is one sure way to overcome them. Overcoming objections involves addressing the concerns or hesitations raised by sellers during the negotiation process. It requires for you to display empathy, problem-solving skills, and the ability to provide reassurance. I want to ensure you that you can anticipate objections because rather you want to believe it or not, they are coming and some stronger than others.

This is not to have you fearful of objections but it is to communicate the truth. I cannot tell you how many times someone told me NO before they gave me a YES! You must understand that for most of the sellers that you are going to contact, you are a complete stranger. You may get 7 No's before they give you 1 Yes... and that's from one client.

Wholesale To Wealth

You have to understand that for the most part you are going to be cold calling. This do not know who you are and neither do they care to know who you are and chances are they had about 200 other people that called them prior to you. Be proactive in identifying potential objections and prepare responses way in advance. You being prepared demonstrates professionalism in such a grand way and you will be rewarded for it!

Cold calling is a sales technique where you are contacting potential customers who have not expressed any prior interest in the product or service being offered. You are reaching out to these prospects via phone or email to introduce your offer and/or service, pitch its benefits, and try to secure a sale or appointment.

So now that you know to expect objections, how do you handle it? One way is to validate the property owners' concerns. Acknowledge the validity of their concerns and show empathy. Empathy is where you put yourself in their shoes for the moment. Showing empathy says that for that quick moment, you feel exactly what they are feeling and you understand.

This helps establish trust and credibility. Do not, I repeat, DO NOT overlook their concerns or belittle them. And do not come off aggressive. Their concerns are valid and should be accepted as such. One of the biggest mistakes is to try to force your will onto a seller. That's one sure way to get hung up on after a few choice words and to get your phone number blocked. Do not come off as if you are the only option. You have to approach the conversation as if you are the best option.

Next you want to offer solutions. Propose practical and reasonable solutions to address their objections. This can help alleviate their concerns and move the negotiation forward. Does the seller have a problem with getting multiple heirs on board such as siblings? Present to the seller a local real estate attorney that specializes in these family type transactions.

Is the seller hesitant because of their age? Then offer the solution of meeting with them and their adult children to go over your offer. If they have a house full of furniture and are boarder line hoarders, then maybe you want to offer a moving company to assist them in relocating. By offering solutions you are presenting this transaction as a win win for all parties and not just yourself.

In the midst of offering solutions, you want to provide evidence or data that supports your position. It's important for you to offer relevant information or data that supports your position or addresses the seller's concerns to build credibility. If the seller has a concern because they had someone who recently promised to buy their home, had it under contract but was not able to close, provide them with proven data of your recent transactions and how you were able to get to the closing table to finalize recent transaction. Just remember to emphasize that you are working together to find a mutually beneficial solution as this reinforces a positive and constructive negotiation environment.

Building rapport, effective communication, active listening, and overcoming objections all contribute to creating a positive and productive negotiation process. These skills will enable you to establish trust, reach favorable agreements, and ultimately, secure profitable deals.

Setting The Appointment

Now that you know how to effectively communicate with the seller, it's time for you to get another step closer to your end goal and that is by setting an appointment. Here you have to be confident in yourself and your abilities to close. It's one thing to talk to someone over the phone, but your mindset have to be that even if they are hesitant over the phone, you know for sure it's a done deal once face to fact.

You don't have to be nervous about this. You are ready! Setting the appointment is actually something you can do on the initial conversation depending on how long and how well the conversation goes. Remember with setting the appointment that you want to ask open ended questions and not close ended questions.

Sample Appointment Setting:

1. So here's the thing. We certainly want to make an offer but I hate do sight unseen offers. So which time works best for me to physically tour the property and then we can further discuss in person our offer? Would today between 12pm-2pm or later in the evening say between 5pm-7pm work best for you?

2. I heard you very clear when you asked how much we are offering. Johnnie to be honest we don't really like to offer sight unseen offers. And this actually benefits both of us. Because honestly the goal is to close and we both would hate to be under contract only for me to discover during our due diligence period that there were some defects I could have discovered simply by conducting a walk-through. So if your schedule permits today, how are you looking around lunch time today?

3. If it's okay with you, I know you mentioned earlier that you were not interested in selling and I appreciate your honesty. If possible I would just like to come tour the home so that I can see what it is that you are looking for in a property and be sure to send you some of the off-market deals we have available.

4. Yes sir! I'm just as excited as you are. Let's get moving. So which day and time works best for this week as I'm flexible?

5. Absolutely! I get it. You have a tenant in the property and you don't want to disturb them. I totally understand. How about we just meet up outside and I will evaluate from the exterior and we go from there. I have some openings in my schedule today anytime between 2pm-4pm. Which time will work best for you?

STAY FOCUS BECAUSE WE UNDERSTAND ITS NOT AN EASY TASK, BUT STAY FOCUS AND KEEP MAKING THE CALLS!

Touring The Property

Congratulations on setting the appointment!!! You are making this look real easy. Now it is time for you to tour the property and then make your offer. Your ability to evaluate the property with eagle eyes is going to help you secure this deal. To be honest you have already done what most would consider is the hard part and that is the phone call. Getting to this step is a major accomplishment so go ahead and pat yourself on the back.

This step here goes great with D's and I's in the DiSC assessment. Now if possible try to tour the property during daylight hours and be sure to avoid late in the evening hours for safety reasons. Also be sure to communicate with an emergency contact your whereabouts. Feel free to drop a pin of your location as you can never be over cautious. Your safety is more important than a transaction.

Prior to taking the drive, feel free to contact the property owner to confirm that they are present or at least in route. One of the worse feelings is showing up to a property, especially in the hood, and the seller says when you call "aww man I thought you were coming tomorrow". So before you leave your residence or office just make a quick phone call to confirm.

Now that you have confirmed, be sure to be on time by being a few minutes ahead of time. Being punctual is important. You want to make sure that you leave to give yourself enough time for traffic and etc. To ensure that you don't run into unexpected traffic, use your GPS or Waze app. Even if you know how to get to the property because you are familiar with the area, still use your GPS or Waze app and communicate if you are running behind schedule.

When you leave out it's ok to send a text of your estimated arrival time to the property. Proper attire and proper hygiene is key. I'm not saying here that you need to wear a suit and tie or dress as there are times I may arrive to a property in my Flip Gang polo shirt, jeans and sneakers. It really depends on the type of property and location of property that may determined that. Or better yet, the brand that you portray.

When I first started out, I was known as the "suit and tie" guy. All I wore was suit and ties, but now it's on a case by case basis. Either way you want to smell good and look good. Now when you arrive to the property be sure to ring the door or knock on the door and step back a couple of steps away from the door.

Greet the owner with a smile and thank them for giving you the opportunity the tour their home. Don't assume that you can just walk in afterwards but ask for permission. Next, ask if they would like to give you a tour or have you walk through freely. Ask if there are any known defects or issues that they would like to disclose.

Starting with the exterior you want to conduct a thorough examination starting with looking at the roof for missing shingles, buckled shingles and even holes in the roof and/or fascia boards. Ask questions about the age of the roof and if there has been any damage to the roof. Look at the brick skirt of the foundation for any cinder blocks that are missing or leaning. You want to take pictures and video of every thing. You want to know if the electrical panel is a 100amp or 200 amp panel. You want to know if the property has or had HVAC systems and if the duct work is in the crawlspace or in the attic.

You want to let the property owner verbally communicate all of the issues as this will help validate your low offer. So point out all issues to the property owner and ask the following questions:

- *Hey Johnnie, how long this water stain been here?*
- *This floor has a serious bounce to it, was there a wall removed or would say that the foundation is starting to give a little and weaken?*
- *What price did you all get to repair all of this if you all were looking to get a major rehab done to this property?*
- *I noticed the air is not on, what are the HVAC issues?*

Notice that all of the questions are open ended. You want to keep the seller talking about the issues that are present. This will encourage them to accept a much lower offer especially if they are aware of the issues and just refused for whatever reason to correct them.

IT'S OFFER TIME

OH IT'S OFFER TIME

YOU'RE MAKING AN OFFER

COME ON!

Making The Offer!

Before taking a tour of the property you should already have some idea of what you're looking to offer especially if you used the price per square feet repair analysis. So your MAO should already be in the back of your head and you are using the physical walk-through as a means to either justify your low offer or to lower your initial offer.

Prior to moving forward with the offer you want to go over your notes by stating back to them the issues that they noted that is wrong with the property. You do not want to present the offer out the gate but try to get the seller to give you a price first. If you are a spades player, then you know not show your hand and not to bid first if you dealt.

Same Offer Script

- *Johnnie, I thank you for allowing me to tour this property. As you stated during our tour this home is close to being a tear down. I do not want to tear it down but I agree that it has some serious issues. Considering everything that this property has going on, what are you really considering for a sales price.*

- *Man I really don't want to disappoint you. I honestly had another number in mind prior to walking through this property but now of course things has changed. We are thinking somewhere in the ball part of $95,000- 105,000. Talk to me about what you think about this offer?*

Put It In Writing and Explain Terms

Now presenting the offer is just the start of this because now that you have presented your offer and negotiated the amount and y'all have agreed, it's time to get it all in writing and outline the terms. Let's say that you both agree to the $98,000. The next thing that you will do is pull out your purchase agreement that you have printed or your lap top to show him electronically. This contract should clearly express your offer. You are not officially under contract until the offer is accepted by the seller in writing.

Verbal acceptances are hard to prove so be sure to get it in writing. Real estate contracts, including assignment contracts, is require to be in writing to be enforceable. You want to make sure that you have clearly articulated the terms that you have in the contract and that the seller clearly understands what you are presenting.

This is important because you are the professional that will be held accountable if things go south. You cannot say "well he/she signed it". That's not how it goes, and if you are a licensed real estate agent, then you really want to make sure that you are communicating throughly along with disclosing your involvement and licensure status.

With a written contract it establishes the mutual agreement necessary for a valid contract. There should be a valuable consideration exchanged, typically in the form of money, to make the contract legally binding but it's not required. Both you and the seller should have the legal capacity to enter into such agreements. This includes being of sound mind and age, and having the authority to represent your respective interests. The language used in the contract should be clear, specific, and unambiguous to avoid misunderstandings or disputes. One of those clauses speaks of your right to assign.

You want to ensure that your contract has a contingency clause with several contingencies such as property inspection, financing, clear title, acceptable rent rolls in rented, and zoning to name a few. This will be your exit strategy in the event that you are not able to find a end-buyer. When it comes to the right to assign you want to make sure that you clearly explain to the seller that you're:

1. *Going to focus on closing on time and them getting the amount that you agreed to.*
2. *Desire the right to assign the contract which means that you have the right to market their property to a database of investors in exchange for an assignment fee.*
3. *Desire to market the property which includes on the MLS with you being the contract owner.*

One of the best things to do is to have a real estate attorney draft your purchase agreement. You do not want to Google Real Estate Wholesale Purchase Agreements and use those as it may be missing some very important information that you need. Schedule a meeting with a local real estate attorney and share what you goals are and if they are willing to be your settlement agent.

Once you and the seller both sign the contract, you are officially under contact and it's now time to get to the next step in the wholesale process.

Remember to have the purchase agreement in your business name and not in your personal name. Try to give yourself 60-90 days to close as you will need all the time the seller will allow.

Marketing and Assigning to End-Buyer

Now that you have the property under contract, its time for you to get to work on getting an end buyer where you are assigning the contract for a profit. Assigning the contract is the process of transferring the rights to purchase a property to your end-buyer in exchange for an assignment fee. This allows you to profit from the difference between the contracted purchase price with the seller and the resale price as long as the seller agreed in writing to you assigning the contact.

The assignment contract should clearly describe the property being assigned, including its address, legal description, and any relevant parcel or lot numbers with a settlement date that is before the settlement date you have with the actual property owner so your contract does not expires with the seller.

If the seller has agreed in writing to allow you to market the property on the MLS, then contact a local real estate agent to list the property on the MLS. Be sure to confirm that your local MLS will allow you to market the property as "contract owner" as this identifies you as not the actual property owner but the contracted owner.

Send a blast out to **The Big 300** letting them know about this now property that you are selling and market this property like non-other. If you have a database of investors, then send them a Google Drive document with great photos and videos of the property. Create a CMA report that shows the ARV along with information of what the comps sold for, days on the market and etc.

Your goal is find a reputable end-buyer who is capable of closing the transaction within the specified time frame with proof of funds. Ensure that the assignment contract is properly drafted, signed by all parties, and legally binding with the original contract with the seller allowing for an assignment. Just a few places to market the property are:

- *Facebook Marketplace and Facebook*
- *Craig's List*
- *All social media platforms and reels*
- *Email your database of investors and realtors*

Once you have a qualified end buyer you want to ensure that they provide proof of funds or a pre-approval letter.

Next Steps After The Assignment Contract

Inform the original seller of the assignment, making it clear that the end buyer will now be completing the transaction with you still as the main contact. Communicate the due diligence process of inspections as well as title search and etc. Next you want to coordinate with your settlement agent. Your settlement agent job is to facilitate the smooth transfer of the contract rights and ensure proper documentation.

Due Diligence Period

Due diligence involves conducting a thorough examination of the legal, physical and intellectual aspects and documentation related to a property. It ensures that the property has clear title and is free from any legal encumbrances along with a property inspection.

Property Inspection

A **property inspection** is the process of thoroughly examining a property to assess its condition, potential repairs, and overall suitability for investment. It involves an inspector inspecting everthing with the interior and exterior of the property. Believe it or not a lot of investors do not conduct a property inspection. But this does not mean that you do not want to get it in writing that they were presented with the opportunity to do so. It's highly advised to always get a property inspection.

This hands-on assessment will consist of the property's structure, systems, and overall condition, providing a detailed understanding of its physical attributes for a set fee that is normally based on the properties square footage or number of units.

Title Search

Once the purchase agreement is ratified, it should immediately be emailed to the settlement company also known as the closing attorney or title company. Their role involves finalizing the transaction and transferring ownership from the seller to the buyer by conducting a thorough title search to verify the property's ownership and identify any outstanding liens or encumbrances. They will offer title insurance to protect both the buyer and seller against potential legal disputes related to the property's title. Some cash buyers may decline title insurance but it's not recommended under any circumstances.

The title company will scrutinize all legal documents related to the property, including deeds, ordering mortgage pay-offs, requesting copies of leases, and any existing contracts or agreements along with acting as the escrow agent.

As the escrow agent their service will have them to act as a neutral third-party intermediary that holds and manages funds, documents, and other assets related to the transaction, along with ensuring that all conditions of the contract are met before the property changes hands.

Zoning and Land Use Compliance

Confirm that the property complies with local zoning and land use regulations. This ensures that it can be used for its intended purpose.

Environmental Assessments

If applicable, conduct environmental assessments to identify any potential environmental hazards or contamination on the property.

Land Survey and Appraisal

Another important part of due diligence is having a surveyor identify and mark the property boundaries using physical markers such as stakes, pins, or monuments. This helps clarify the legal boundaries of the property and prevent any boundary disputes in the future especially with neighbors.

An appraisal provides an objective assessment of the property's value, ensuring fair and accurate valuations as may be required by certain lenders if the buyer is receiving financing for the purchase.

Finalizing the Transaction

Review Closing Documents

Now it's time for you to get paid. The due diligence process has ended and the buyer is willing to move forward. This is even better if the buyer did not try to get a price reduction during the due diligence period. The first document you should request and review from the settlement company is the ALTA.   This document will show all of the numbers and one of the main lines you are looking for is to confirm that your assignment fee is on the ALTA and correct.

Next all parties including should review and sign the necessary closing documents, including the deed, mortgage note, and any additional paperwork required by the title company or escrow service along with the buyer bringing the necessary funds to closing.

Recording of Documents and Transfer of Funds

The deed and other relevant documents are recorded with the appropriate county or municipal office to officially transfer ownership of the property. The title company or escrow agent disburses the funds to the seller, covering the purchase price, any outstanding debts, and fees associated with the transaction and to you as the wholesaler.

Once the documents are recorded, the buyer officially becomes the legal owner of the property and you are on to your next deal.

If you are a licensed real estate agent this is where you may have the opportunity to get paid again by assisting the buyer will reselling the property after they rehab it.

Wholesaling Extras

Now that you have a few deals under your belt, I think it's time for you to consider scaling your business and here are some ways for you to scale your business so that you are taking your business to another dimension. Scaling your business involves leveraging automation, building a strong network, and strategically expanding into new markets. These steps can help you increase deal volume, profitability, and overall business success.

Lead Generation Automation

This involves leveraging technology and systems to consistently and efficiently identify and qualify potential real estate deals. The use of CRMs (Customer Relationship Management) are designed to manage leads, track interactions, and automate follow-up communications.

There are several CRM software options that are popular and well-suited for you to choose from to implement in you business. This is not in any specific order but just a few.

Podio: A customizable CRM platform that allows you to organize leads, track deals, and collaborate with team members. It offers features such as task management, workflow automation, and integration with other tools.

InvestorFuse: Helps streamline lead management, automate follow-ups, and track deal progress. InvestorFuse also offers customizable workflows and integrations with popular real estate tools.

PropStream: Offers lead generation, property analysis, marketing tools, skip tracing and CRM features to manage leads, track deals, and communicate with prospects.

REIvolution: Offers lead management, deal tracking, automated follow-ups, and marketing tools to streamline the wholesaling process.

InvestorPO: Provides lead management, deal tracking, email marketing, and reporting features to help wholesalers manage leads and close deals efficiently.

These are just a few examples of CRMs that are popular among real estate wholesalers. It's important to consider factors such as ease of use, customization options, integration capabilities, and pricing when choosing a CRM for your wholesaling business. Additionally, some CRMs offer free trials or demos, allowing you to test the platform before committing to a subscription.

Online Marketing and Advertising

Utilize digital marketing platforms, such as social media, Google Ads, and targeted email campaigns, to reach a wider audience and generate leads. This will include the use of SEO (search engine optimization) and content marketing which optimizes your website for search engines to attract organic traffic. It' important that you are creating valuable content that resonates with your target audience of buyers and sellers and encourages those who are not to refer.

Collaborate with Realtors

Build relationships with real estate agents who can provide leads and opportunities for wholesaling deals. Agents provide valuable insights, resources, and assistance to your network, demonstrating your expertise and commitment to their success.

Expand into New Markets

Now that you mastered your area, its time to start expanding into new markets. This involves venturing into different geographic areas or niches within the real estate market to increase your deal volume and potential profitability.

Conduct thorough research to identify promising markets based on factors like demand, property values, and economic indicators. Establish local connections by building relationships with local real estate professionals, including realtors, investors, and property managers, to gain insights and access to potential deals.

Tailor your marketing efforts to cater to the specific needs and preferences of the new market. This may include adjusting messaging, targeting, and channels. Start with smaller, low-risk projects in the new market.

End-of-Course Quiz Question

1: The seller agrees to sell 123 N Main St for $265,000. It is 1,800 sq ft and needs cosmetic repairs. Using the formula in this guide and with you wanting to net a $10,000 assignment fee, what is the least amount you can assign this property to a end-buyer for?

A) $337,850 B) $347,000 C) $275,000 D) $266,800

Question 2: What is the ARV if the following comps sold for $255,000, $263,500, $261,000 and $259,000?

A) $261,600 B) $259,625 C) $259,500 D) $1,038,500

Question 3: As a wholesaler you are required to get an home inspection on the property prior to assigning it to the end buyer?

A) YES, because you must disclose all property defects B) YES, if you are a licensed real estate agent C) NO D) YES

Question 4: Which of the following is an ethical consideration in skip tracing?

A) Conducting skip tracing without obtaining consent B) Using public databases for skip tracing C) Verifying information through multiple sources D) Charging a fee for skip tracing services

Question 5: What is a common objection that sellers may raise during negotiations in real estate wholesaling?

A) Requesting a higher purchase price B) Expressing eagerness to close the deal quickly C) Offering additional properties for sale D) Expressing gratitude for the offer

Question 6: What is one of the key components of a brand?

A) Unique Selling Proposition (USP) B) Competitor Analysis C) Market Segmentation D) Marketing Budget

Question 7: What is a primary benefit of automating lead generation in real estate wholesaling?

A) Reducing the need for networking B) Increasing the number of potential leads C) Eliminating the need for due diligence D) Decreasing the quality of leads

Question 8: What role does a title company play in closing a real estate deal?

A) Conducting property inspections B) Facilitating the transfer of funds and legal documents C) Determining repair costs D) Negotiating with the seller

Question 9: What is a key consideration when expanding a wholesaling business into new markets?

A) Ignoring local regulations B) Adapting marketing strategies to the new market C) Avoiding networking in the new area D) Implementing the same strategies as in the original market

Question 10: What is a critical component of effective communication in negotiations?

A) Providing vague information to keep the seller guessing

B) Using complex jargon to impress the seller C) Responding to objections with pre-prepared scripts D) Clarity and conciseness in conveying information

Answers

1. C) $275,000

2. B) $259,625

3. C) NO

4. A) Conducting skip tracing without obtaining consent

5. A) Requesting a higher purchase price

6. A) Unique Selling Proposition (USP)

7. B) Increasing the number of potential leads

8. B) Facilitating the transfer of funds and legal documents

9. B) Adapting marketing strategies to the new market

10. D) Clarity and conciseness in conveying information

Mastering Scripts

If you are going to be successful at wholesaling you must master scripts. I cannot emphasize how important it is for you to practice. I personally have been practicing for years and I still do. No one should be practicing on real clients. You should have partners that you role play with to help you get used to using the scripts along as it will help you with overcoming objections as well minimizing hmms and ahhhs.

Start salutation with enthusiasm:

Great morning/afternoon! This is (YOUR NAME) with (YOUR COMPANY) and I'm looking to speak with the property owner of (PROPERTY ADDRESS). Are you the property owner?
Great! May I have your name please, just to confirm that I have the right information in our database?

If you are using a skip tracing platform or some type of software that pulls public information never assume that the database have the correct name. Always ask for a name so that you are confirming what you have because if you start out with the name and its incorrect they will quickly say "wrong number" and hang up. Also you want to make sure that you are displaying enthusiasm, as it has a way of communicating confidence. The goal is to bring them up to your level and not the other way around. Expect them to be a little distant especially if you're contacting someone that is delinquent on their mortgage. Remember you will get better with time, but mastering the opening is crucial to your overall success so PRACTICE IT.

Sample Questions to Ask:

Thank you (THEIR NAME) for taking my call. I'm not trying to keep you long so I will try to make this as quick as possible. The reason why I am calling is because we are a group of investors in the area and I just wanted to speak with you in regards to your property and just had a few questions for you.

The worst thing someone can say is NO. So if that is the worst thing they can say then why are you not making the calls?

Don't be lazy and don't be afraid of rejection. Rejection like resistance helps build muscle.

- We noticed that the sellers in your area have been taking advantage of this moving market and wanted to know your thoughts on taking advantage as well?

- Are you currently living in this property or is it occupied by a tenant?

- To be totally honest, we are interested in purchasing your property and wanted to know your thoughts on reviewing offers?

- One of our core values is creating win win solutions where it's not one sided. So is there any specific concerns you have with selling your property that we may address?

These are just some starter questions to break the ice with. You can expect the seller to be combative if they are not really looking to sell.

Objections to Expect

When you start making calls, you can expect objections. But you can also master overcoming objections. You don't have to quickly give in and hang up the phone. I want you to read the following objections and then thank of ways for you to overcome them without ignoring them.

Below are just a few objections that you can expect to hear when contacting property owners. All of them are valid responses to you calling them out of the blue to purchase their property that they for the most part was not even looking to sell. You must be mindful not to take anything personal. Understand that your number one job is to build rapport. Hitting a home run on the first pitch and first swing is highly unlikely, but if you keep stepping up to the plate and you continue to swing, eventually you will rock it out the park. Don't get frustrated!

Wholesale To Wealth

- I'm not interested
- How did you get my number
- Why do you all keep calling my phone
- I'm not looking to sell my home so don't call me
- Do you know what time it is why are you calling me this early
- We don't have any place to go to if we sell this home
- I have to talk to my wife/husband about it
- My home is already under contract
- My best friend is an agent so if I'm looking to sell I will use her
- Just send me over an offer and if I'm interested I will call you back
- If you are not going to pay me top dollar then there is no need for us to talk any further

IT'S TIME
FOR YOU
TO GO
BE GREAT
AND HAVE
FUN DOING
IT!

DOMENICK EPPS
REAL ESTATE INVESTOR, BROKER & AUTHOR

Born and raised in the Saratoga community of Suffolk, VA. Married to his lovely wife LaKita "Queen" Epps they are blessed with daughters Morgan, Trinity, Zoey, Shakima and son Domenick Epps Jr. Domenick has 15+ years of real estate investing experience and 10+ years as a licensed real estate agent. Domenick currently resides in the Atlanta, GA metro area where he is continuing to teach and pour into others.